Crafts
from your favorite
Bible Stories

Crafts
from your favorite
Bible Stories

By Kathy Ross

Illustrated by Sharon Lane Holm

Christian Crafts

The Millbrook Press   Brookfield, Connecticut

For all the children of the Gethsemane Church
sunday school, Sherrill, New York.
K.R.

For Zoe Elizabeth, welcome little one.
S.L.H.

Library of Congress Cataloging-in-Publication Data
Ross, Kathy (Katharine Reynolds), 1948–
Crafts from your favorite Bible stories / by Kathy Ross ; illustrated by Sharon Lane
Holm.
p.   cm. —(Christian crafts)
Summary: Presents instructions for making twenty-seven craft projects related to Bible
stories and characters including a Jonah in the whale puppet, a cardboard tube
manger, and a hair-growing Samson.
ISBN 0-7613-1619-1 (lib. bdg.) — ISBN 0-7613-1295-1 (pbk.)
1. Bible crafts Juvenile literature. [1. Bible crafts. 2. Handicraft.] I. Holm, Sharon Lane,
ill. II. Title. III. Series: Ross, Kathy (Katharine Reynolds), 1948– Christian crafts.
BS613.R67   2000   268'.432—dc21   99-26864   CIP

Published by The Millbrook Press, Inc.
2 Old New Milford Road
Brookfield, Connecticut 06804
www.millbrookpress.com

38, 478 X

Contents

Introduction

Proverbs 22.6 says: "Train up a child in the way he should go, and when he is old he will not depart from it."

Sharing the wonderful stories of the Bible with children has surely been one of the more rewarding and fruitful joys in my life. To pass on the stories of struggle and triumph, of faith and miracles, and of God's love for us is essential to building character and to establishing the framework of Christian understanding at an early age.

My many years of working with and training children in preschool and Sunday school have shown me that involving them in stories strengthens their understanding. The hands-on experiences of making and using props related to Bible stories have been invaluable in helping children to remember the stories as well as to understand their underlying message.

This book shares with you and your children some of my favorite Bible stories and the projects I used to teach them. I hope that they will enrich your child's Bible study, as they have the many children I have been blessed to share them with over the years.

Happy crafting,

Kathy Ross

The story of how God created the world and everything in it is told in the very first chapter of the first book of the Bible (Genesis 1:1).

Creation Wheel

you need:

scissors

pencil

ruler

corrugated cardboard

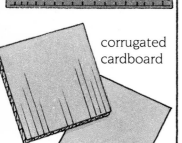

light-weight cardboard

markers

white glue

cotton ball

paper fastener

what you do:

1 Cut a 12-inch (30-cm) circle from the corrugated cardboard. Cut an identical circle from the light-weight cardboard.

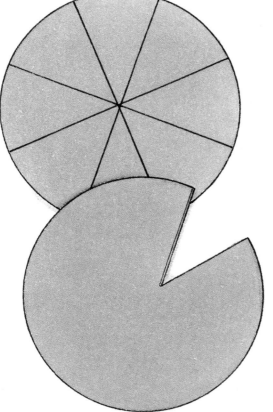

2 Use the ruler to divide the corrugated cardboard circle into eight equal wedge-shaped segments. Cut a segment from the light-weight cardboard that is slightly smaller than one segment of the corrugated cardboard circle. Make sure it does not go all the way to the center of the light-weight cardboard circle.

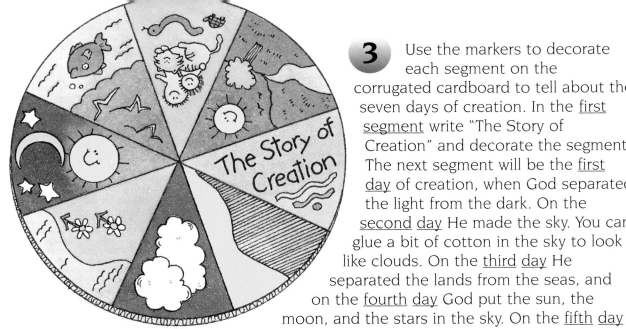

3 Use the markers to decorate each segment on the corrugated cardboard to tell about the seven days of creation. In the <u>first segment</u> write "The Story of Creation" and decorate the segment. The next segment will be the <u>first day</u> of creation, when God separated the light from the dark. On the <u>second</u> day He made the sky. You can glue a bit of cotton in the sky to look like clouds. On the <u>third day</u> He separated the lands from the seas, and on the <u>fourth day</u> God put the sun, the moon, and the stars in the sky. On the <u>fifth day</u> He filled the seas with fish and the sky with birds. On the <u>sixth day</u> He created all the animals and He created man. On the <u>seventh day</u> God rested from his work.

4 Attach the light-weight cardboard circle to the top of the corrugated cardboard circle by putting the paper fastener through the center of both circles. Arrange the top circle so that the title segment, "The Story of Creation," shows through.

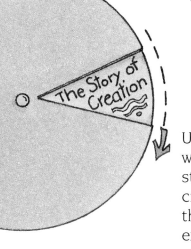

Use the creation wheel to tell the story of the creation, turning the top wheel to expose the picture of each of the seven days.

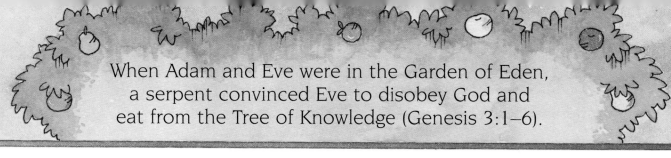

The Tree of Knowledge

you need:

four 12-inch (30-cm) brown pipe cleaners

scissors

scrap of orange paper

ruler

12 small red beads

one 12-inch (30-cm) green pipe cleaner or sparkle stem

white glue

green yarn

Styrofoam tray to work on

green poster paint and a paintbrush

cardboard egg carton

black sharp-pointed marker

what you do:

1 Fold three of the brown pipe cleaners in half. Twist them together above the folded ends to form a tree trunk, with the ends of the pipe cleaners fanning out to form the branches of the tree. Cut the last brown pipe cleaner into 1-inch (2.5-cm) pieces. Wrap the pieces around the branches of the tree to make smaller branches.

2 Slip the beads onto the branches to look like fruit on the tree.

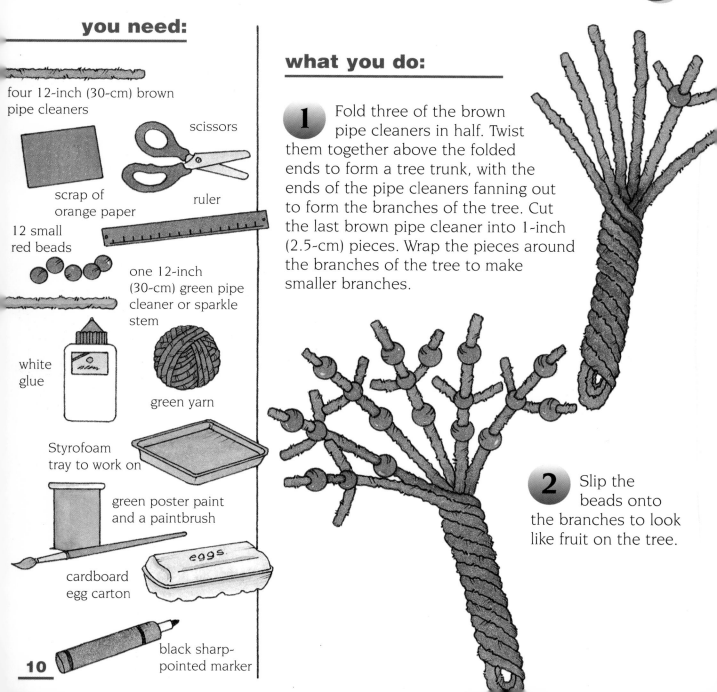

3 Wrap the branches of the tree with green yarn to look like the leaves. Tie one end of a long piece of yarn to a branch, then weave it in and out through the branches until the branches are all entwined. When you like the way the tree looks, trim off any extra yarn and tie the end to a branch to secure it.

4 Cut a cup from the cardboard egg carton and paint it green. Let it dry. Turn the cup over and poke a hole in the center to slip the base of the tree through to make a stand for the tree.

5 Wrap the green sparkle stem around the base of the tree to look like the serpent. Cut two tiny eyes for the serpent from the orange paper scrap. Use the black marker to put a pupil in the center of each eye. Glue the eyes to the end of the green sparkle stem.

The serpent reminds us of the consequences of disobeying God!

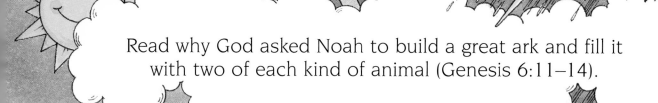

Read why God asked Noah to build a great ark and fill it with two of each kind of animal (Genesis 6:11–14).

Noah's Ark

you need:

two 9-inch (23-cm) uncoated paper plates

scissors

markers

white glue

colored construction paper for animals

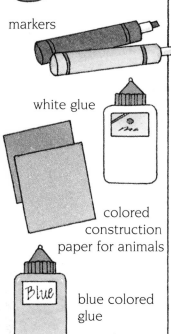

blue colored glue

paper fastener

what you do:

1 Fold one plate in half so that you know where the center is located. Cut the plate into two pieces about 1/2 inch (1.25 cm) off center so that one piece is about 1 inch (2.5 cm) bigger than the other piece.

2 Color the two pieces with the markers, then glue them together, eating sides in, to form the boat.

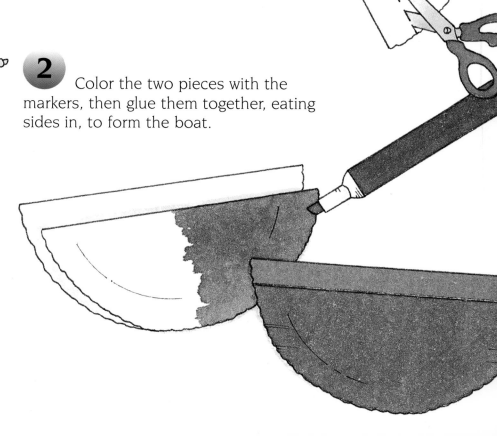

3 Cut animals from the construction paper to put in the ark. Don't forget to make two of each animal. Use markers to add details to the animals.

4 Draw a line across the center of the second paper plate. Use the markers to color a storm scene on one half of the plate. If you wish you can put raindrops on your storm scene using drops of blue glue. Turn the plate upside down and color a rainbow in a blue sky with a dove carrying an olive branch on the other half.

5 Use the paper fastener to attach the center of the boat to the center of the back plate.

Put your animals on board. To change the scene from the forty days of rain to the promise of dry land, turn the back plate around. God keeps His promises.

God keeps His promise to Abraham
and his wife Sarah and gives them a baby, Isaac,
in their old age (Genesis 18:9–10).

Sarah and Baby Isaac Puppet

you need:

scissors

pink and white felt scraps

markers

white glue

old mitten

ruler

piece of fabric big enough to wrap around mitten

what you do:

1 From the pink felt, cut a circle for Sarah's face. Make the circle about as wide as the top of the mitten you are using. Draw a face on the felt circle using the markers. Glue the face to the top, palm side of the mitten.

2 Cut a tiny circle about as wide as the thumb of the mitten for the baby's face. Use the markers to draw on facial features. Glue the face to the top of the thumb of the mitten.

3 Cut a 3-inch (8-cm) triangle from the white felt for the baby's blanket. Wrap it around the thumb of the mitten with the baby's face peeking out. Glue the blanket in place.

4 Cut a rectangle of fabric large enough to wrap around the mitten and base of the thumb for Sarah's clothes. Wrap it around the mitten with the face peeking out and glue the fabric to the mitten.

To use the puppet slip your hand into the mitten and wiggle the little baby Isaac that Sarah is holding in her arms.

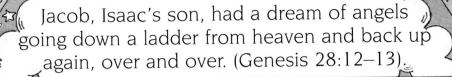

Jacob, Isaac's son, had a dream of angels going down a ladder from heaven and back up again, over and over. (Genesis 28:12–13).

Jacob's Ladder

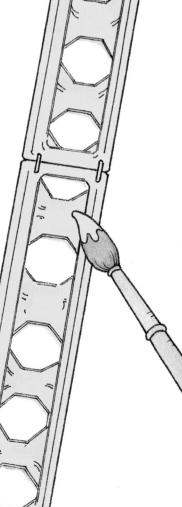

you need:

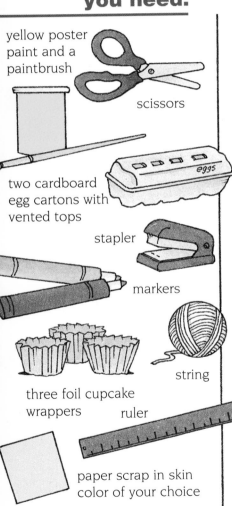

yellow poster paint and a paintbrush

scissors

two cardboard egg cartons with vented tops

stapler

markers

string

three foil cupcake wrappers

ruler

paper scrap in skin color of your choice

three yellow paper cupcake wrappers

newspaper to work on

what you do:

1 Cut the long vented center out of the lid of each egg carton. Staple the two strips together at the center to form a ladder.

2 Paint the ladder yellow and let it dry.

3 To make each angel, fold a foil cupcake wrapper in half, then fold the two sides back over each other to make a dress.

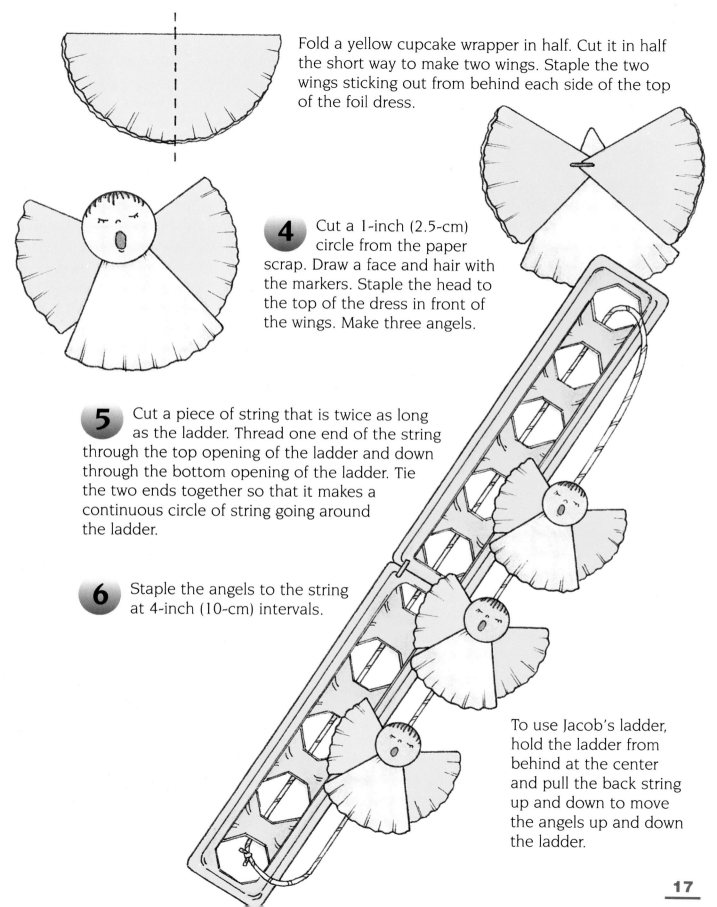

Fold a yellow cupcake wrapper in half. Cut it in half the short way to make two wings. Staple the two wings sticking out from behind each side of the top of the foil dress.

4 Cut a 1-inch (2.5-cm) circle from the paper scrap. Draw a face and hair with the markers. Staple the head to the top of the dress in front of the wings. Make three angels.

5 Cut a piece of string that is twice as long as the ladder. Thread one end of the string through the top opening of the ladder and down through the bottom opening of the ladder. Tie the two ends together so that it makes a continuous circle of string going around the ladder.

6 Staple the angels to the string at 4-inch (10-cm) intervals.

To use Jacob's ladder, hold the ladder from behind at the center and pull the back string up and down to move the angels up and down the ladder.

Jacob favored his son Joseph and gave him a colorful coat that made his brothers jealous (Genesis 37:3–4).

Joseph Magnet

you need:

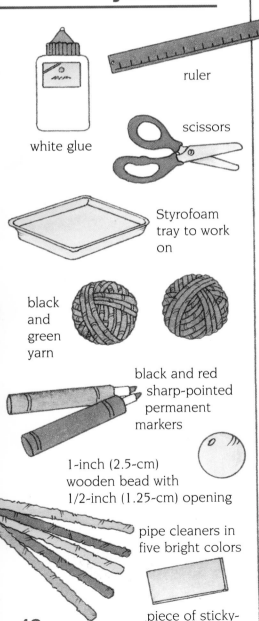

white glue

ruler

scissors

Styrofoam tray to work on

black and green yarn

black and red sharp-pointed permanent markers

1-inch (2.5-cm) wooden bead with 1/2-inch (1.25-cm) opening

pipe cleaners in five bright colors

piece of sticky-backed magnet

what you do:

1 Trim five different colored pipe cleaners to a length of 8 inches (20 cm). Bunch the pipe cleaners together and fold them in half. Dip the folded end in glue and stick it into the hole in the bead. The bead will be the head and the pipe cleaners the colorful coat. Trim the bottom of the pipe cleaners to even them out.

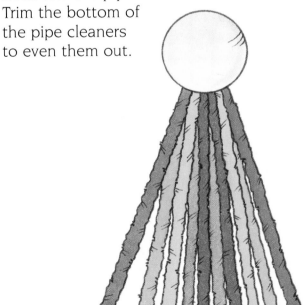

2 Cut one 3-inch (8-cm) piece from each of three different colored pipe cleaners for the sleeves of the coat. Slide them up between the pipe cleaners, forming the coat, and glue them in place. Tie a belt of green yarn around the coat just below the arms to help secure them.

3 Use the markers to draw a face on the bead. Glue on bits of black yarn for the hair.

4 Press a piece of sticky-backed magnet on the back of the pipe-cleaner coat and hang the project on your refrigerator.

Joseph is a wonderful reminder that even when things seem hopeless, God is there with a plan to make things right for us.

milk
dog bones
bread

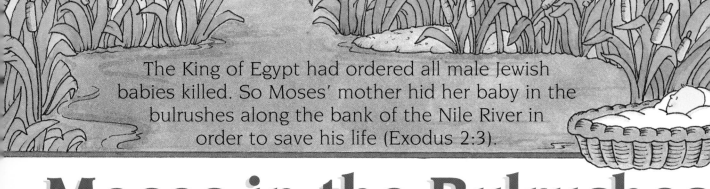

The King of Egypt had ordered all male Jewish babies killed. So Moses' mother hid her baby in the bulrushes along the bank of the Nile River in order to save his life (Exodus 2:3).

Moses in the Bulrushes Glove Puppet

you need:

scissors

cardboard egg carton

yellow poster paint

paintbrush

felt in blue, white, brown, and skin color

white glue

black yarn

two small wiggle eyes

old knit glove

newspaper to work on

what you do:

1 Cut one egg cup from the egg carton. Cut a hole through one side of the bottom of the cup large enough to put your finger through. Paint the cup yellow and let it dry. This will be the basket for baby Moses.

2 From the blue felt, cut a pool of water that is wider than the glove. Cut a slit across the middle of the pool and slide it over the fingers and thumb of the glove so that the water surrounds them.

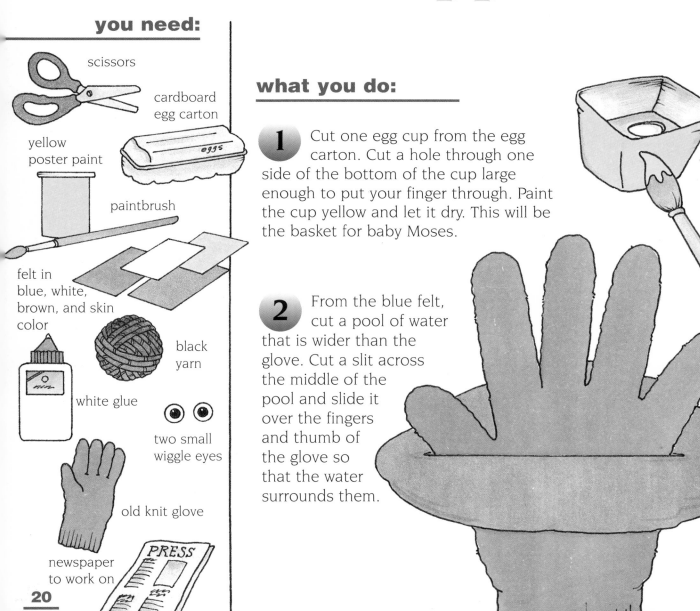

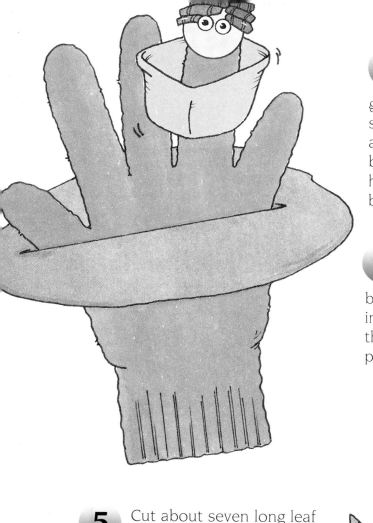

3 Slide the basket down over one of the middle fingers of the glove. Cut a 1-inch (2.5-cm) circle of skin-color felt for the head of the baby and glue it to the tip of the finger in the basket. Glue yarn bits to the top of the head for hair. Glue two wiggle eyes below the hair.

4 Cut a square of white felt for a blanket. Glue the blanket in the egg cup so that only the baby's eyes are peeking out.

5 Cut about seven long leaf shapes from the brown felt for the bulrushes that grew in the river. Glue them on the fingers and in the water so that the basket looks like it is floating among them.

To use the glove puppet put your hand in and wiggle your fingers to bob baby Moses up and down in the water among the bulrushes. God took care of Moses.

Among the many miracles God performed for His people was the parting of the waters of the Red Sea to let them escape from slavery (Exodus 14:26–27).

The Parting of the Red Sea

you need:

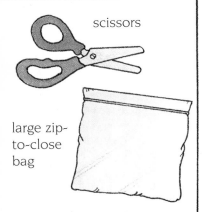

scissors

large zip-to-close bag

stapler

white glue

light-weight cardboard

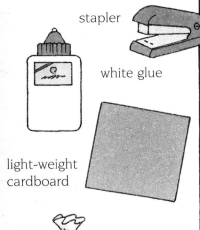

sand

blue plastic wrap

BLUE PLASTIC

what you do:

1 Carefully cut down the two sides of the zip-to-close bag and open it out flat.

2 Cut a square of light-weight cardboard that will fit exactly in the center of the flattened bag and allow the bag to fold up over each side of the cardboard and zip closed. Staple the cardboard to the plastic bag.

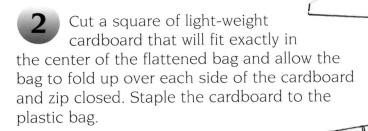

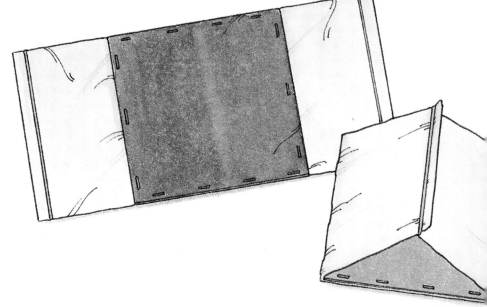

3 Cover the cardboard with glue, then sprinkle it with sand to look like the bottom of the sea. You may want to add some cut-out starfish or seashells.

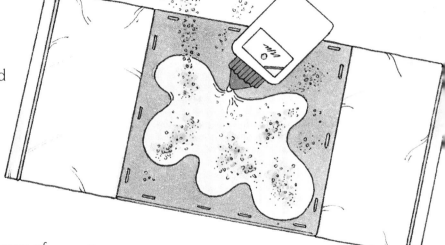

4 Crumble several squares of blue plastic wrap to fit over the flap of plastic bag on each side of the ocean bottom. Attach the crumbled pieces to the inside and outside of the bag flaps using a stapler to hold them in place. Use just enough pieces to cover the flaps. If you make it too thick the two flaps will no longer meet and close over the sandy bottom. Do not staple too close to the zipper.

Close the waters over the sandy bottom by zipping the two sides together. Show how the waters parted for Moses and the Israelites, then closed again once they were safely across.

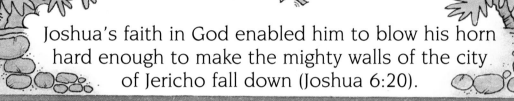

Joshua's faith in God enabled him to blow his horn hard enough to make the mighty walls of the city of Jericho fall down (Joshua 6:20).

Ram Horn Trumpet

you need:

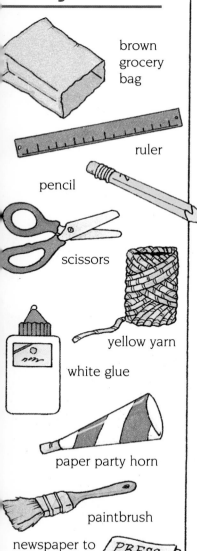

brown grocery bag

ruler

pencil

scissors

yellow yarn

white glue

paper party horn

paintbrush

newspaper to work on

what you do:

1 Cut a 12-inch (30-cm) square piece from the brown bag.

2 Use the paintbrush to spread white glue all over one side of the square.

3 Starting at one corner, roll the square around the party horn and into a cone shape, trimming off any excess.

4 Bend the wide end of the cone shape up about one-third of the way from the end. Let it dry completely to be sure the bent shape will hold.

5 Cut a 3-foot (90-cm) length of yarn and tie each end around the horn as shown so you can carry it over your shoulder.

Blow the horn and imagine you are helping to make the walls of Jericho fall down.

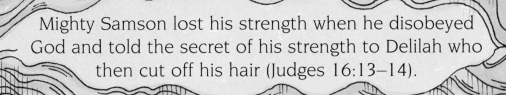

Mighty Samson lost his strength when he disobeyed God and told the secret of his strength to Delilah who then cut off his hair (Judges 16:13–14).

Hair-Growing Samson

you need:

pencil

construction paper in skin color

white glue

markers

cardboard toilet-tissue tube

scissors

cardboard egg carton

dirt

Styrofoam egg carton

grass seed

water

what you do:

1 Draw a body for Samson on the construction paper as tall as the cardboard tube. Do not draw a head on the body. Use the markers to draw on clothes. Cut out the body and glue it to one side of the cardboard tube.

2 Cut a cup from the cardboard egg carton for the head. Use markers to draw a face on one side of the head, with the open end of the cup up.

3 Glue the head to the top of the body.

4 Cut a cup from the Styrofoam egg carton. Put it inside the cardboard cup head for a liner.

5 Fill the head with dirt and sprinkle with grass seed. Don't forget to water the seed lightly every few days.

Can you put Samson in a sunny window and help him grow his hair back?

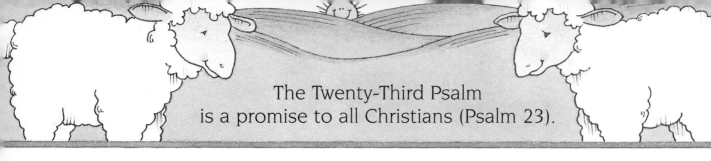

The Twenty-Third Psalm
is a promise to all Christians (Psalm 23).

Hand Lamb

you need:

white crayon

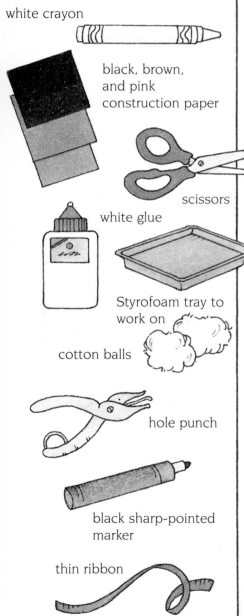

black, brown, and pink construction paper

scissors

white glue

Styrofoam tray to work on

cotton balls

hole punch

black sharp-pointed marker

thin ribbon

what you do:

1 Use the white crayon to trace around your hand on the black paper. Cut the hand shape out.

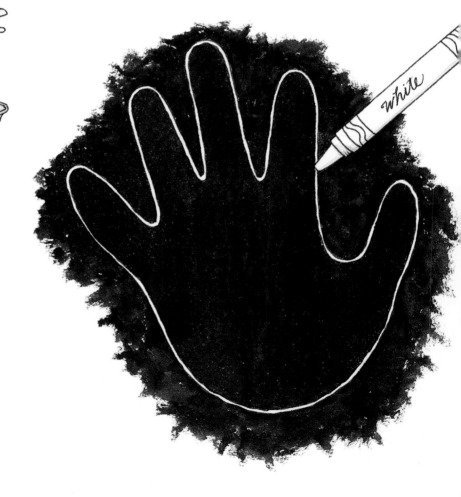

white

2 Cover the palm of the hand and the base of the thumb and fingers with glue. Then attach cotton balls to make a sheep.

3 Punch an eye for the sheep from the brown paper. Use the black marker to draw a dot in the center of the eye for a pupil. Glue the eye to the middle of the thumb.

4 Tie a piece of thin ribbon around the base of the thumb to form a neck for the sheep. Tie the ribbon in a bow.

5 Cut a heart shape from the pink paper small enough to fit on the back of the sheep. Write "The Lord is my shepherd" and "Twenty-Third Psalm" on the heart with the marker. Glue the heart to the reverse side of the sheep.

The Lord is my shepherd. Psalm 23

This psalm tells us that God loves us and will take care of us.

God sent ravens to feed
the prophet Elijah (I Kings 17:4).

Elijah and the Ravens Puppets

you need:

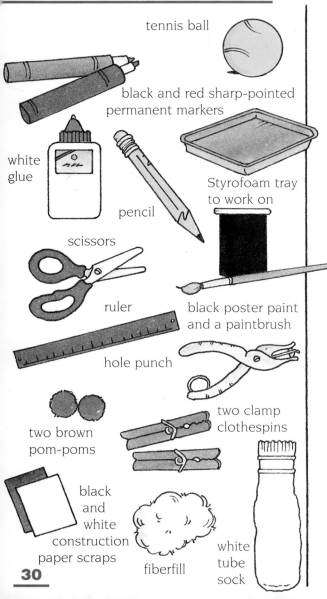

tennis ball

black and red sharp-pointed
permanent markers

white glue

pencil

Styrofoam tray to work on

scissors

ruler

black poster paint and a paintbrush

hole punch

two brown pom-poms

two clamp clothespins

black and white construction paper scraps

fiberfill

white tube sock

what you do:

1 Ask a grown-up to cut a 2-inch (5-cm) slit across one side of the tennis ball for a mouth for the puppet. You will also need a 1-inch (2.5-cm) slit cut in the bottom side of the ball to attach the body of the puppet.

2 Use the red marker to draw lips around the puppet's mouth. Draw the rest of the face with the black marker.

3 Glue on hair and a beard made from fiberfill—or you can make a shorter beard from cotton.

4 Trim the cuff of the tube sock so that you are left with a sock about 11 inches (28 cm) long. Use the pencil to help you stuff the toe of the sock into the slit in the bottom of the ball.

5 Draw arms and other details of the robe with the black marker.

6 The two clothespins will be the ravens. Paint them black and let them dry on the Styrofoam tray.

7 Cut wings for each bird from the black paper. Glue the wings on one side of each clothespin.

8 Punch out two eyes for each bird from the white paper. Use the black marker to draw a dot in the middle of each eye for a pupil. Glue the eyes to the top bar of each clothespin toward the clamp end.

9 To feed Elijah, put a pom-pom in each raven's mouth to represent the bread and the meat sent to Elijah by God. Hold each side of the head and squeeze to make the mouth open. Fly each raven to Elijah and squeeze the back of the clothespin to release the food into Elijah's mouth.

God will take care of you, too.

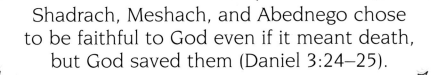

Shadrach, Meshach, and Abednego chose
to be faithful to God even if it meant death,
but God saved them (Daniel 3:24–25).

Shadrach, Meshach, and Abednego in the Fiery Furnace

you need:

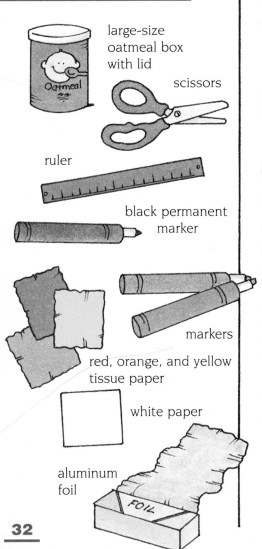

large-size oatmeal box with lid

scissors

ruler

black permanent marker

markers

red, orange, and yellow tissue paper

white paper

aluminum foil

what you do:

1 Cut off the top portion of the oatmeal box so that you are left with the box about 6 inches (15 cm) tall. Turn the box over to use to make the furnace.

2 Cut a rounded door out of one side of the box, leaving one side attached to the box to serve as a hinge so that the door will open and close. Close the door and put the lid over the cut portion of the box to form the bottom of the furnace. You will need to trim off some of the bottom part of the door so that it will open and close without getting caught on the lip of the lid.

3 Cover the entire box, including the door, with aluminum foil. Use the black marker to draw the outline of stones over the outside of the furnace.

4 Cut a 12-inch (30-cm) square of tissue paper in each of the three colors. Tuck the tissue into the furnace to look like flames.

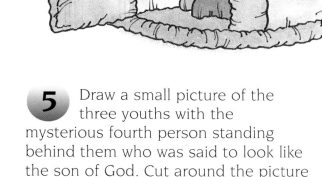

5 Draw a small picture of the three youths with the mysterious fourth person standing behind them who was said to look like the son of God. Cut around the picture and tuck it into the furnace.

Whenever you open the door to look in the furnace you will remember what great and amazing miracles happen when we have faith.

Only Daniel could tell the King
the meaning of the mysterious
handwriting on the wall (Daniel 5:25).

The Handwriting Appears on the Wall

you need:

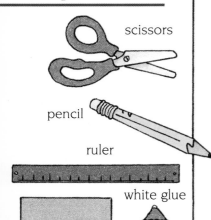

scissors

pencil

ruler

white glue

12- by 18-inch (30- by 46-cm) sheet of construction paper in wall color

marker

construction paper in skin color

what you do:

1 Cut a 3- by 18-inch (8- by 46-cm) strip off the bottom of the construction paper you are using for the wall.

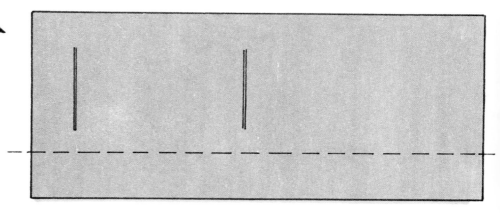

2 Cut a 4-inch (10-cm) slit up the middle of one side of the larger sheet of paper. Cut a parallel slit about 9 inches (23 cm) to the left of the first cut.

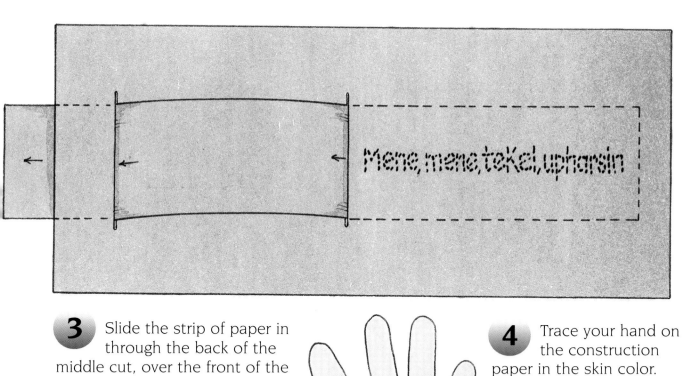

3 Slide the strip of paper in through the back of the middle cut, over the front of the paper, and through the cut on the edge. When the paper is exactly lined up behind the larger sheet, the wall should look blank.
On the part of the paper that is hidden behind the larger paper write *Mene, mene, tekel, upharsin*, which was a warning to the evil king.

4 Trace your hand on the construction paper in the skin color. Cut out the hand outline. Glue the hand to the paper on the wall so that the fingers cover the center slit in the paper.

To make the hand look like it is writing a warning on the wall, slowly pull the smaller paper to one side to reveal the hidden message.

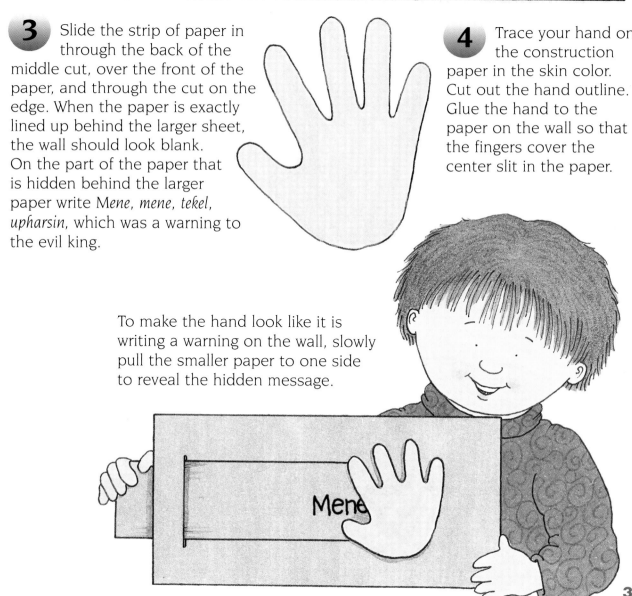

35

Jonah was thrown off a boat in a stormy sea and spent three long days in the belly of a big fish (Jonah 1:17).

Jonah in the Big Fish Puppet

you need:

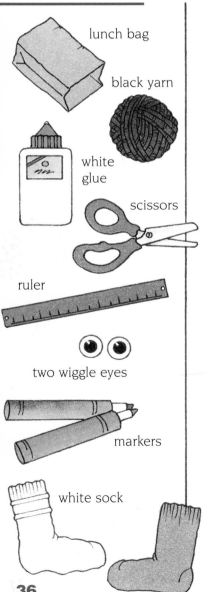

lunch bag

black yarn

white glue

scissors

ruler

two wiggle eyes

markers

white sock

brown sock

what you do:

1 To turn the lunch bag into a big fish cut a triangle out of the open end to form a tail. Cut an opening across the bottom of the bag and about 1 inch (2.5 cm) up each side to make the open mouth of the big fish. Use markers to draw on eyes and any other details you might want to add.

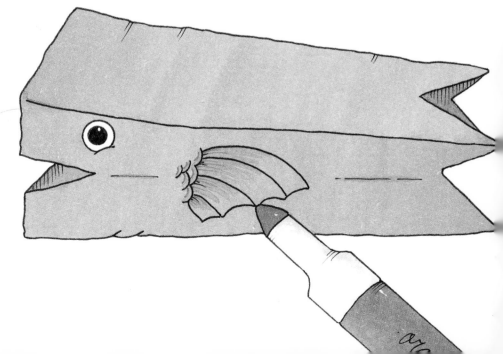

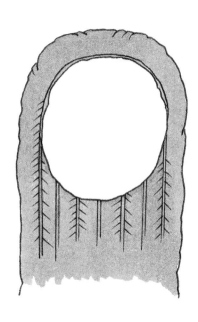

2 To make Jonah, cut a 2-inch (5-cm) circle out of the top of the toe of the brown sock. Put the white sock inside the brown sock so that the white shows through as the head of Jonah and the brown sock as his clothing.

3 Cut bits of black yarn and glue them on for the hair and the beard. Glue on the two wiggle eyes, or use buttons if you prefer.

4 The Jonah puppet goes on your hand and arm. If the socks seem too long just cut the bottoms off to a length that is comfortable for you.

To use your puppet, first put Jonah on your hand, then put your hand in through the back of the big fish so that Jonah peeks out of the mouth.

Jonah had a hard time learning to obey God!

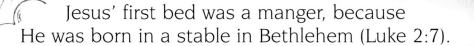

Jesus' first bed was a manger, because
He was born in a stable in Bethlehem (Luke 2:7).

Cardboard Tube Manger

you need:

scissors

white glue

four card-
board
wrapping-
paper tubes
of similar
width and
length

twine

large sheet
of brown poster
board

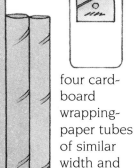

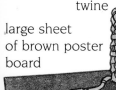

newspaper
to work on

what you do:

1 Glue two of the cardboard tubes together in an X shape, with the centers crossing over each other. Glue the second pair of tubes in an X shape that exactly matches the first set of tubes. These will be the legs of the manger.

2 When the glue has dried, wrap twine around the meeting point of the two tubes of each leg to give the legs a rustic look. Trim off any extra and slip the end under the twine layers and tie it to keep it in place.

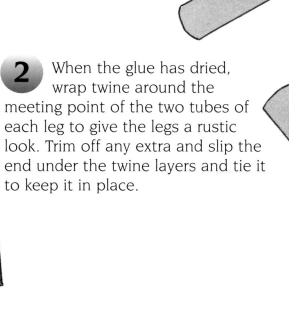

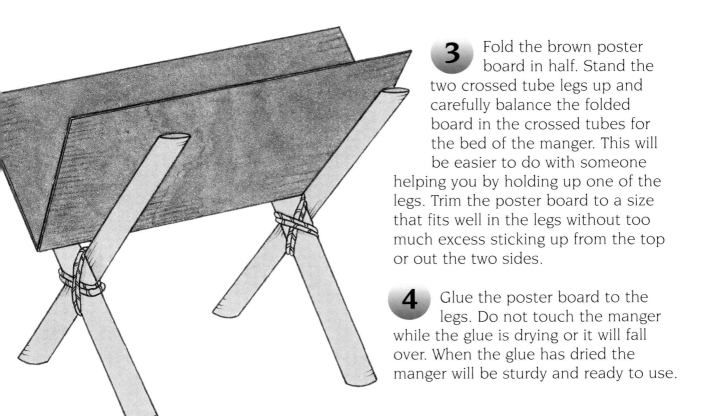

3 Fold the brown poster board in half. Stand the two crossed tube legs up and carefully balance the folded board in the crossed tubes for the bed of the manger. This will be easier to do with someone helping you by holding up one of the legs. Trim the poster board to a size that fits well in the legs without too much excess sticking up from the top or out the two sides.

4 Glue the poster board to the legs. Do not touch the manger while the glue is drying or it will fall over. When the glue has dried the manger will be sturdy and ready to use.

You might want to put some yellow yarn in the manger for hay and wrap up a baby doll to be the baby Jesus. Not only is the manger a reminder of whose birthday we celebrate at Christmas, but it can also be used to play with as you act out the Christmas story.

The three kings found the baby Jesus by following a bright star (Matthew 2:9–11).

Three Kings Hats

you need:

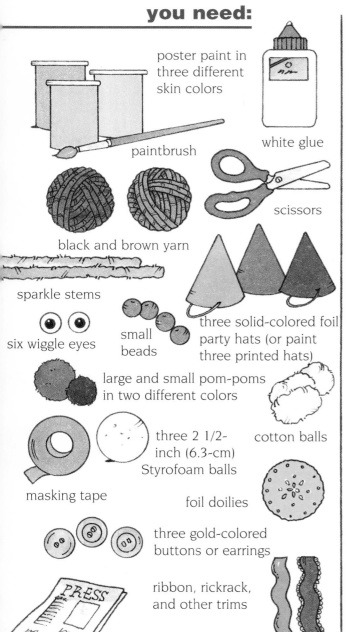

poster paint in three different skin colors

paintbrush

white glue

scissors

black and brown yarn

sparkle stems

six wiggle eyes

small beads

three solid-colored foil party hats (or paint three printed hats)

large and small pom-poms in two different colors

cotton balls

masking tape

three 2 1/2-inch (6.3-cm) Styrofoam balls

foil doilies

three gold-colored buttons or earrings

ribbon, rickrack, and other trims

newspaper to work on

what you do:

1 Paint each of the three Styrofoam balls a different skin color. Let the paint dry.

2 Press a head over the point of each hat. Slip the heads off again. Cover each point with glue and put the heads back on.

3 The hats will be the gowns of the kings. Decorate the gowns with pieces of the foil doilies and different trims. Make each king look different. For a gift, attach a gold button or earring to the front of each king, using a piece of rolled masking tape.

4 Glue on a pair of wiggle eyes for each king. Use the cotton and the black and brown yarn to give each king a different color hair and beard.

5 Use pieces of sparkle stem with beads strung on to make a crown for one of the kings. Use rickrack for another. Give the third king a hat by gluing the large pom-pom topped by the small pom-pom on top of his head.

These kings look as good standing on a table as they do on your head.

We can still find Jesus in our world today.

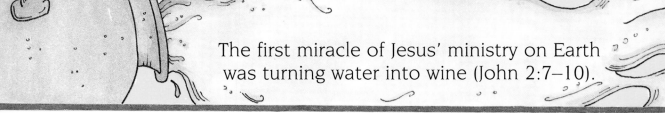

The first miracle of Jesus' ministry on Earth was turning water into wine (John 2:7–10).

Turning Water Into Wine

you need:

ruler

scissors

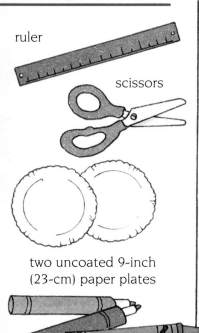

two uncoated 9-inch (23-cm) paper plates

red, blue, and green markers, crayons, or paints

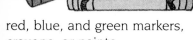

brown construction paper

white glue

paper fastener

what you do:

1 Cut a curved section about 1 1/2 inches (3.75 cm) wide and 6 inches (15 cm) long just below the rim of one of the plates. Color the top (eating side) of the plate green.

2 Hold the cutout plate over the second plate. Use a blue marker to trace around the cutout portion of the first plate on the second plate. Color the traced portion and the area around it blue.

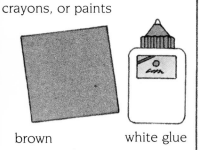

Blue

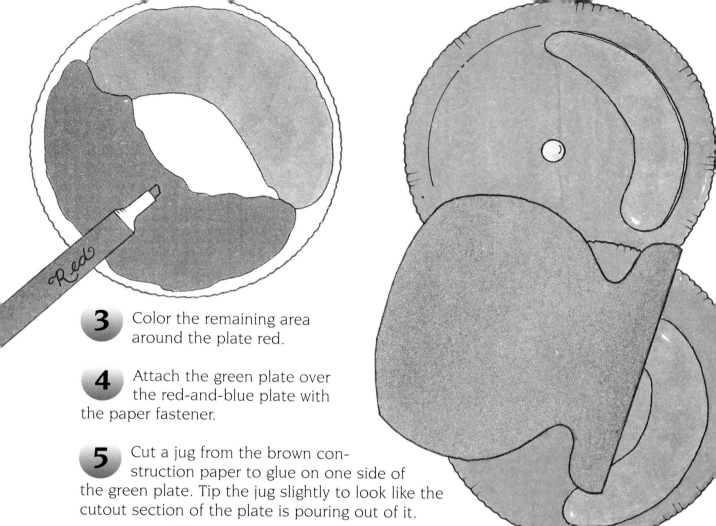

3 Color the remaining area around the plate red.

4 Attach the green plate over the red-and-blue plate with the paper fastener.

5 Cut a jug from the brown construction paper to glue on one side of the green plate. Tip the jug slightly to look like the cutout section of the plate is pouring out of it.

To show Jesus' first miracle start the wheel with the blue showing to represent water flowing from the jug. Slowly turn the back plate to change the blue water to red wine by revealing the red portion of the colored plate.

Jesus told a crippled man that his sins were forgiven, and the man stood up and walked (Mark 2:11–12).

Stand Up and Walk

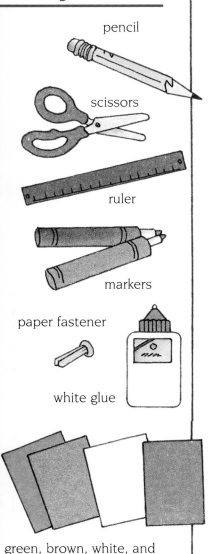

pencil

scissors

ruler

markers

paper fastener

white glue

green, brown, white, and orange construction paper

what you do:

1 Cut a 4- by 10-inch (10- by 25-cm) rectangle from the brown paper for a bed for the crippled man.

2 From the white construction paper, cut the shape of a man with his feet slightly apart. Make him a size that will fit on the bed.

Use markers to give the man a face, hair, and a beard. Cut a garment for the man from the orange paper. Trace around the outside of the figure to get a good fit. Glue the garment on the man.

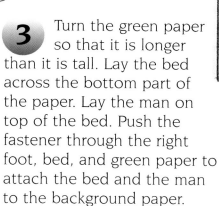

3 Turn the green paper so that it is longer than it is tall. Lay the bed across the bottom part of the paper. Lay the man on top of the bed. Push the fastener through the right foot, bed, and green paper to attach the bed and the man to the background paper.

To show what happened when the crippled man listened and trusted in Jesus, stand the man up by swinging the figure on the fastener. Then swing the bed up and tuck it under his arm.

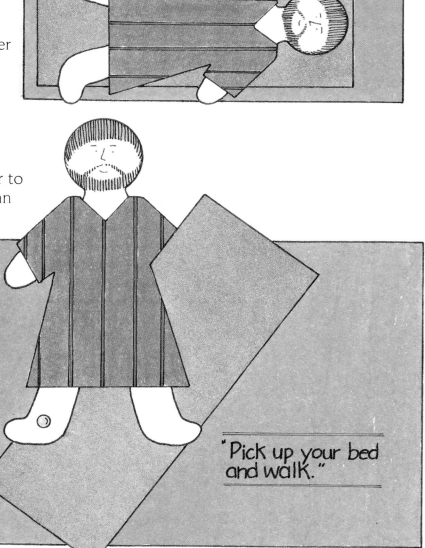

"Pick up your bed and walk."

Jesus miraculously feeds 5,000 people with only 5 loaves of bread and two fishes (Matthew 14:17–20).

A Basket With Five Loaves and Two Fishes

you need:

yellow poster paint

paintbrush

uncoated 9-inch (23-cm) paper plate

yellow yarn

scissors

ruler

hole punch

brown marker

white glue

brown and gray construction paper

newspaper to work on

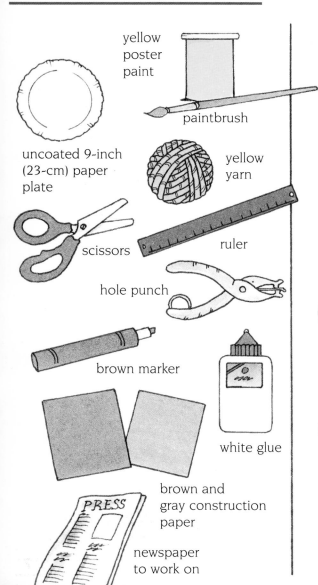

what you do:

1 Paint (or color) both sides of the paper plate yellow.

2 Cut four equally spaced 2-inch (5-cm) slits around the plate.

3 Punch a hole at the corner of both sides of two sections of the plate that are directly across from each other.

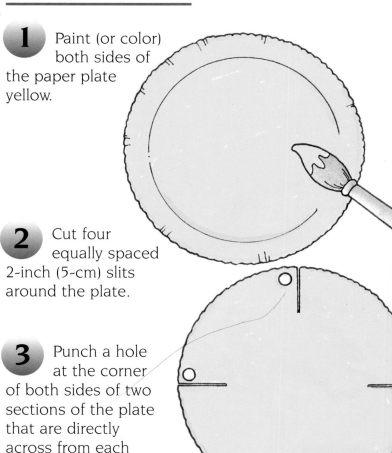

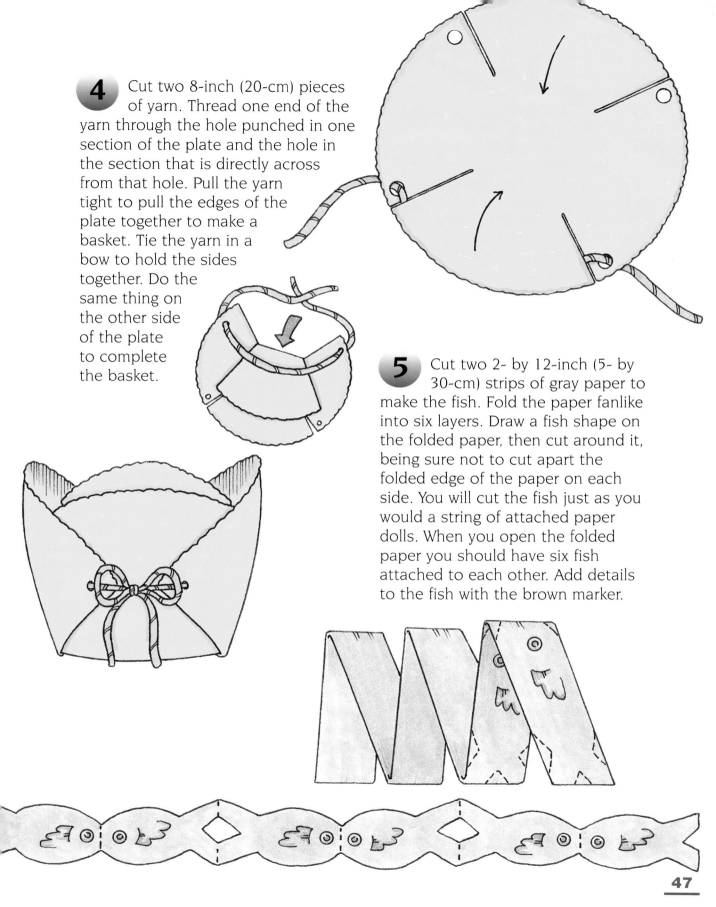

4 Cut two 8-inch (20-cm) pieces of yarn. Thread one end of the yarn through the hole punched in one section of the plate and the hole in the section that is directly across from that hole. Pull the yarn tight to pull the edges of the plate together to make a basket. Tie the yarn in a bow to hold the sides together. Do the same thing on the other side of the plate to complete the basket.

5 Cut two 2- by 12-inch (5- by 30-cm) strips of gray paper to make the fish. Fold the paper fanlike into six layers. Draw a fish shape on the folded paper, then cut around it, being sure not to cut apart the folded edge of the paper on each side. You will cut the fish just as you would a string of attached paper dolls. When you open the folded paper you should have six fish attached to each other. Add details to the fish with the brown marker.

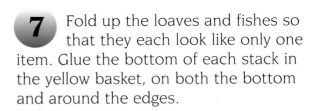

6 To make the loaves of bread cut five 2- by 12-inch (5- by 30-cm) strips of brown paper. Fold the paper fanlike into six layers. Draw the shape of a loaf of bread on the top layer, then cut it out, being sure not to cut apart the folded edge of the paper on each side.

7 Fold up the loaves and fishes so that they each look like only one item. Glue the bottom of each stack in the yellow basket, on both the bottom and around the edges.

To show how Jesus turned five loaves and two fishes into enough to feed 5,000 people, unfold the loaves and fishes to turn a little food into a lot. Sometimes we think we do not have what we need, but Jesus shows us we have more than enough.

Jesus brings a little girl back to life
(Mark 5:41–42).

Jairus's Daughter Puppet

you need:

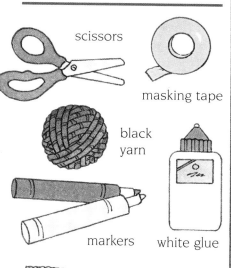

scissors

masking tape

black yarn

markers   white glue

white tube sock

pink construction paper

fabric scrap

salt box with metal pouring spout

shoe-box lid

what you do:

1 Cut the top off the salt box about 1 inch (2.5 cm) below the top.

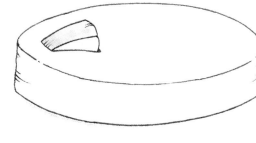

2 Cover the metal spout with masking tape to create a better gluing surface

3 Color the top of the box with a marker in skin color for the face of the girl. Draw on facial features with markers, placing the eyes on either side of the spout as shown. Make sure to draw the eyes wide open.

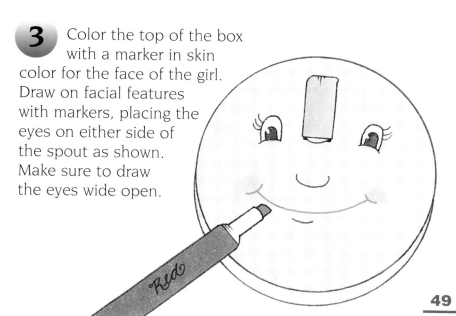

4 Cut two attached eyelids from the pink paper to cover the eyes to make them look closed. Cut several 1-inch (2.5-cm) pieces of yarn and glue them along the bottom of each lid to look like eyelashes. Glue the center of the eyelids to the spout of the salt box. By pushing on the back of the spout you should now be able to open the eyes. Be careful of the back of the metal spout, it might be sharp. Use a piece of fabric to push on it to protect your fingers.

5 Cut bits of yarn for hair and glue them around the head.

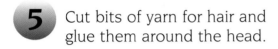

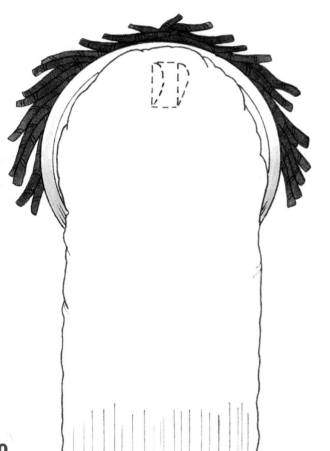

6 Glue the head to the top, toe end of the sock. Be careful not to block your access to the back of the salt spout with too much gluey sock. Cut some sock away if needed.

7 Cut a hole in the center of the shoe-box lid large enough to put your hand through. Put the cuff of the sock down through the hole from the inside of the lid so that the head lies on the box lid like it is a bed. Trim off any excess sock that hangs down below the foot of the box-lid bed when you hold it upright.

8 Cut a square of fabric for a blanket. Put glue only over the inside of the shoe-box lid below the hole, even though the blanket comes up over the hole. Glue the bottom portion of the blanket in the box.

To show what Jesus did for the little girl, put your hand up inside the sock and push the back of the spout to open her eyes. Tip your hand forward to make her sit up and look around. What a wonderful story!

One night Jesus walked across the water to His disciples. But when Peter tried to walk out to meet Him, his faith was overcome by fear and he sank (Matthew 14:28–30).

Jesus Walks on Water

you need:

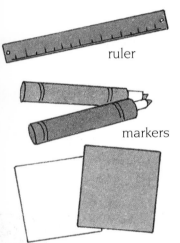

ruler

markers

white and brown construction paper

scissors

white glue

two 9- by 12-inch (23- by 30-cm) sheets of blue construction paper

what you do:

1 Draw a 5-inch (13-cm)-tall picture of Jesus and of Peter on the white construction paper to use in your scene. Think about how Jesus might look and feel as He walks across the water full of faith and how Peter would feel as he begins to doubt God and sinks. Cut out the two figures.

2 Cut a shape to represent the front of the boat from the brown construction paper. Make it about 3 inches (8 cm) tall and 5 inches (13 cm) long. Glue the end of the boat to the right side of the paper.

3 Cut a 6-inch (15-cm) slit across the blue paper, starting from the middle of the top of the boat and going toward the center of the paper out of the boat.

4 Glue the cut paper with the boat on it over the second sheet of blue paper, being careful to glue only around the edges of the paper so that you do not glue the slit shut.

5 Glue Jesus in the upper left corner of the paper walking on the water toward the boat. Slip Peter into the boat by sliding him into the slit.

To show what happened, pull Peter up to the top of the slit to move him out of the boat and onto the water. After he is on the water, slide him down into the slit in the paper to make it look like he is sinking in the water.

Jesus wants us to trust in Him.

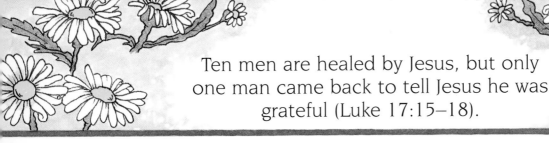

Ten men are healed by Jesus, but only one man came back to tell Jesus he was grateful (Luke 17:15–18).

A Story About Gratitude

you need:

12- by 18-inch (30- by 46-cm) sheet of white construction paper

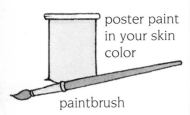

poster paint in your skin color

paintbrush

markers

newspaper to work on

what you do:

1 Fold the white sheet of paper in half so that you have a 9- by 12-inch (23- by 30-cm) card that opens from the top.

2 Paint your hands, one at a time, and print them on the front of the paper.

3 Open the paper up carefully so you do not smear the handprints (or wait until they are dry) and print your two fists inside the paper. To do this, close the fingers of your hand and paint over the palm and knuckles, then press the closed hand on the paper. You will need to roll the closed hand back and forth a bit to paint the entire area to look like a fist.

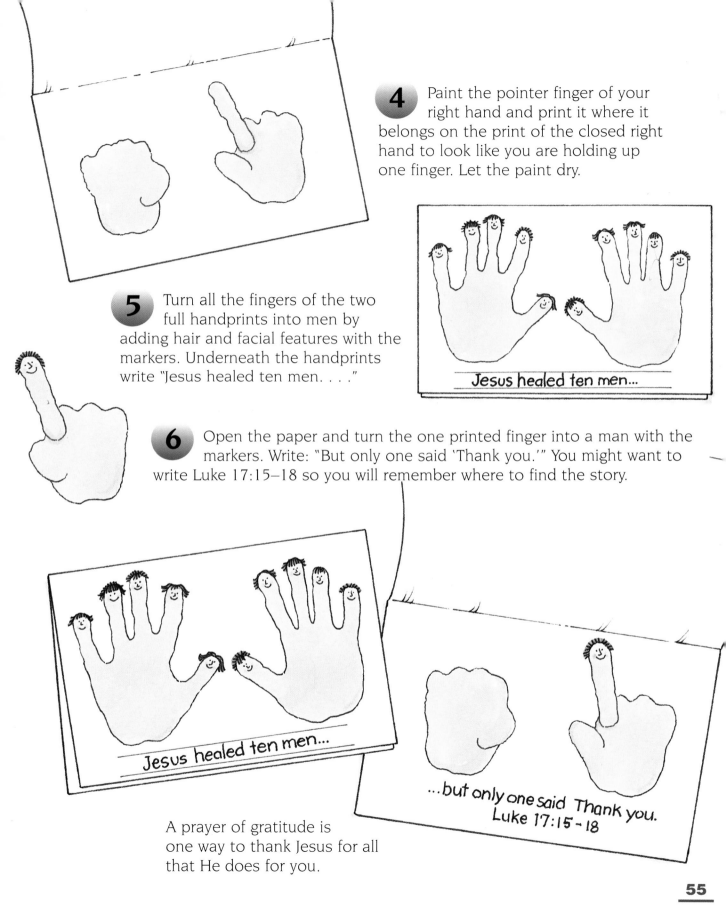

4 Paint the pointer finger of your right hand and print it where it belongs on the print of the closed right hand to look like you are holding up one finger. Let the paint dry.

5 Turn all the fingers of the two full handprints into men by adding hair and facial features with the markers. Underneath the handprints write "Jesus healed ten men. . . ."

Jesus healed ten men...

6 Open the paper and turn the one printed finger into a man with the markers. Write: "But only one said 'Thank you.'" You might want to write Luke 17:15–18 so you will remember where to find the story.

Jesus healed ten men...

...but only one said "Thank you."
Luke 17:15-18

A prayer of gratitude is one way to thank Jesus for all that He does for you.

The people of Jerusalem welcomed Jesus with palm branches (Matthew 21:8–9).

Waving Palms

you need:

scissors

markers

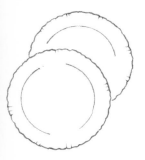

two uncoated 9-inch (23-cm) paper plates

paper fastener

what you do:

1 Cut a half-circle piece out of the inner rim of one plate that does not quite go all the way to the middle of the plate.

2 Use the markers to draw a person below the cut opening of the plate. The hands of the person should reach up to the opening. Also color in the background around the person.

3 Use the paper fastener to attach the center of the cut plate over the center of the second plate.

4 Draw a curved palm on the exposed area of the bottom plate in each hand of the person.

5 Carefully turn the back plate in one direction and extend the drawing of the palms on the exposed portion of the back plate. Turn the plate in the other direction and do the same thing. Color the area around the palms blue for sky.

6 Write: "Hosanna! Blessed is He who comes in the name of the Lord" above the palms.

Turn the back plate back and forth to show the person waving palms in celebration of Jesus' arrival.

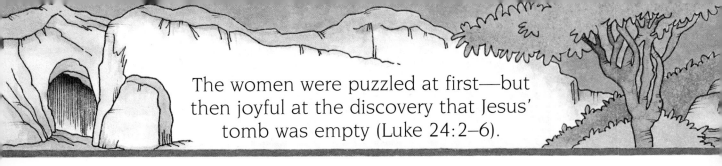

The women were puzzled at first—but then joyful at the discovery that Jesus' tomb was empty (Luke 24:2–6).

The Empty Tomb

you need:

scissors

markers

stapler

masking tape

piece of light-weight cardboard about 10- by 12-inches (25- by 30-cm)

paper fastener

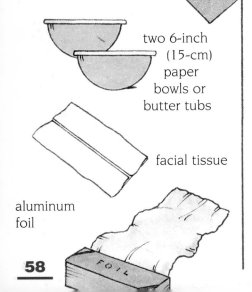

two 6-inch (15-cm) paper bowls or butter tubs

facial tissue

aluminum foil

what you do:

1 Cut a rounded cave opening through the lower right side of the cardboard that is slightly smaller than the inside of the bowls.

2 Color the cardboard around the cave opening to look like an outdoor scene.

3 Cover the inside of one of the bowls by wrapping it with aluminum foil.

4 Staple the bowl to the back of the cardboard to form the inside of the cave. Crumple a piece of foil to make a shelf of rock inside the cave. Use masking tape to attach the shelf to the floor of the cave. Cut a 2- by 6-inch (5- by 15-cm) strip of tissue to look like the empty shroud. Use masking tape to attach the shroud to the rock shelf.

5 Cover the bottom of the second bowl with aluminum foil to make the rock in front of the cave opening. Attach the edge of the bowl to the cardboard on the left side of the cave opening using the paper fastener. Roll the stone away from the cave on the paper fastener to reveal the empty tomb.

The Lord has risen indeed! Alleluia!

Jesus appeared to His followers many times in the 40 days after His crucifixion, and then was seen rising up to heaven (Acts 1:9).

Jesus Ascends

you need:

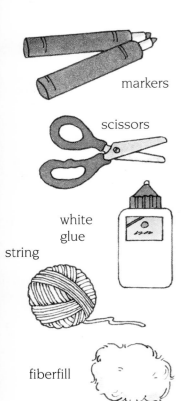

markers

scissors

white glue

string

fiberfill

sliding matchbox

what you do:

1 Slide the inner box out of the matchbox. Use the markers to draw a picture of Jesus on the bottom of the box.

2 Poke a small hole through the side of the box above the head of the drawing.

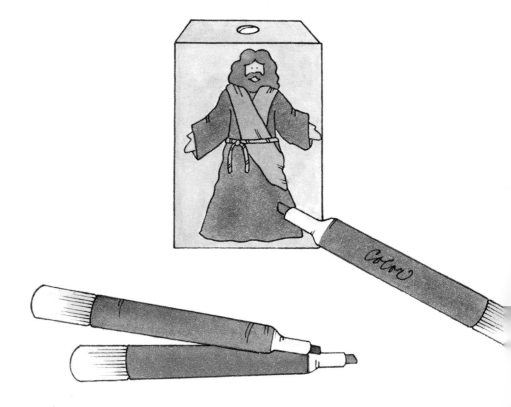

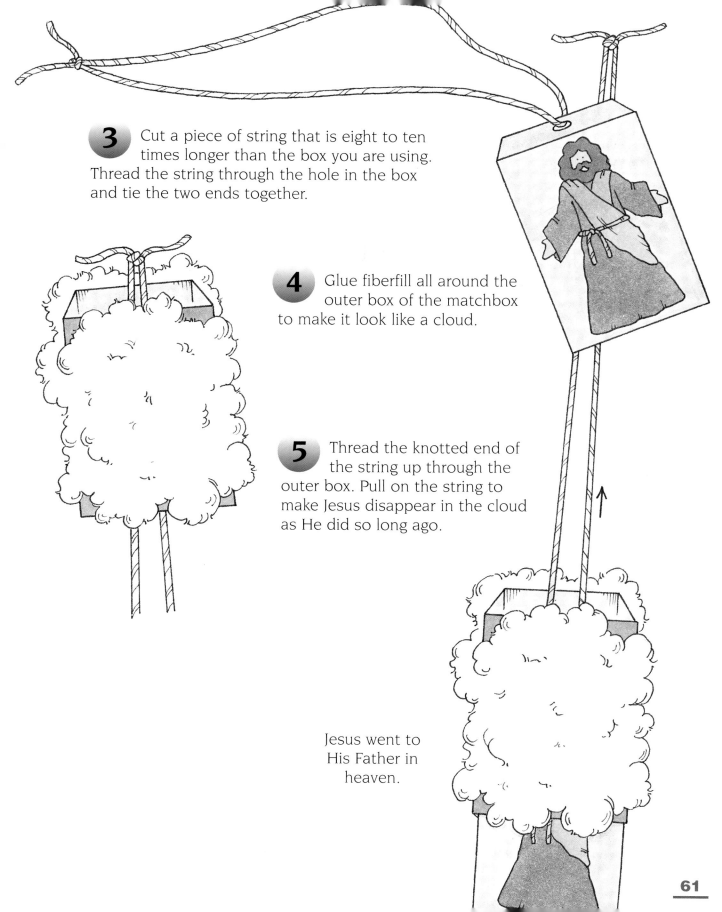

3 Cut a piece of string that is eight to ten times longer than the box you are using. Thread the string through the hole in the box and tie the two ends together.

4 Glue fiberfill all around the outer box of the matchbox to make it look like a cloud.

5 Thread the knotted end of the string up through the outer box. Pull on the string to make Jesus disappear in the cloud as He did so long ago.

Jesus went to His Father in heaven.

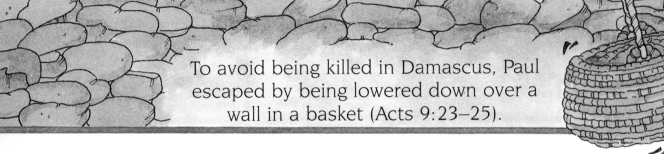

To avoid being killed in Damascus, Paul escaped by being lowered down over a wall in a basket (Acts 9:23–25).

Paul Over the Wall

you need:

markers

white glue

scissors

black yarn

hole punch

12-inch (30-cm) brown pipe cleaner

two cardboard paper-towel tubes

plastic berry basket

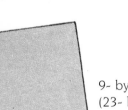

large cork

9- by 12-inch (23- by 30-cm) piece of lightweight cardboard

what you do:

1 Use a marker to draw the outline of stones all over one side of the cardboard to make it look like a wall.

2 Glue a cardboard tube on the back of each side of the wall to make the wall stand up.

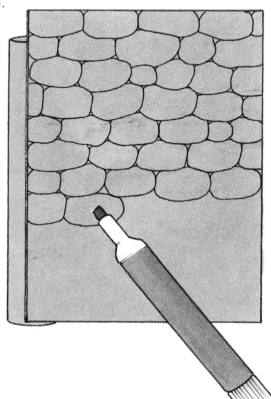

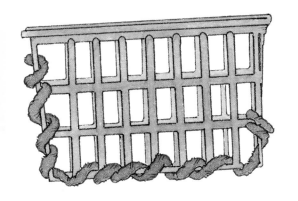

3 To make the basket in which Paul can escape, cut two sides from the berry basket, leaving them attached at the corner. Fold the two sides in together and weave the brown pipe cleaner in and out to close the bottom and open side. Trim off any extra pipe cleaner.

4 Cut two pieces of yarn, each twice as long as the height of the wall. Punch two holes in the top of the wall the same distance apart as the width of the basket. Thread one of the pieces of yarn through one side of the basket. Thread both ends of the yarn through the hole at the top of the wall directly above that side of the basket. Do the same thing with the second piece of yarn on the other side of the basket. Tie the four ends of yarn together behind the wall. You should now be able to move the basket up and down the wall by pulling and releasing the knotted ends of yarn behind the wall.

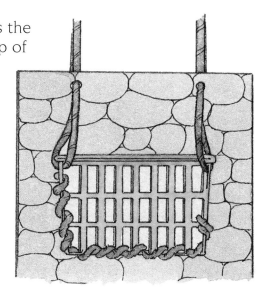

5 Use markers to color the cork to look like Paul. Put the cork into the basket.

Quick! Help Paul escape from Damascus by lowering him down over the wall in the basket!

About the Author and Illustrator

Twenty-five years as a Sunday school teacher and director of nursery school programs has given Kathy Ross extensive experience in guiding young children through craft projects. Among the more than 30 craft books she has written are GIFTS TO MAKE FOR YOUR FAVORITE GROWNUP, CRAFTS FROM YOUR FAVORITE FAIRY TALES, and CRAFTS FOR ALL SEASONS.

Sharon Lane Holm, a resident of Fairfield, Connecticut, won awards for her work in advertising design before shifting her concentration to children's books. Among the books she has illustrated recently are SIDEWALK GAMES AROUND THE WORLD and HAPPY BIRTHDAY, EVERYWHERE!, both by Arlene Erlbach, and BEAUTIFUL BATS by Linda Glaser.

Together, Kathy Ross and Sharon Lane Holm have also produced the popular *Holiday Crafts for Kids* series as well as the *Crafts for Kids Who Are Wild About* series.